MY FAMILY IS DRIVING ME CRAZY!

My Family Is Driving Me Crazy!

Buster Soaries

VICTOR BOOKS®
A DIVISION OF SCRIPTURE PRESS PUBLICATIONS INC.
USA CANADA ENGLAND

Scripture quotations, unless otherwise indicated, are from the *Holy Bible, New International Version,* © 1973, 1978, 1984, International Bible Society. Used by permission of Zondervan Bible Publishers. Quotations marked KJV are from the King James Version.

Thought and discussion questions prepared by Lin Johnson.

Library of Congress Cataloging-in-Publication Data

Soaries, Buster.
My family is driving me crazy / by Buster Soaries.
p. cm.—(Straight Talk series)
Summary: A Christian guide to building a positive atmosphere of communication and support in the family.
ISBN 0-89693-939-1
1. Teenagers—Conduct of life. 2. Communication in the family—Juvenile literature. [1. Family life. 2. Christian life.]
I. Title. II. Series.
BJ1661.S64 1991
158′.24–dc20 91-15461
CIP
AC

---

1 2 3 4 5 6 7 8 9 10 Printing/Year 94 93 92 91

This book is dedicated to my mother and the memory of my father. They provided me with all of my basic tools and my fondest memories.

ACKNOWLEDGMENTS

This book would have never been completed had my wife, Donna, not been there to encourage and prod me when I thought I would never actually finish the work. I thank God for giving me the best wife in the world. The fact is that Jane Vogel at Victor Books has been committed to helping me publish a book for the past four years. Her friendship, patience, persistence, and support made this dream become a reality.

Also the following persons were invaluable in their assistance: Terri Soaries and Regina Plunkett at the Soar! Corporation; and Judy Presley, Margaret Bascome, Anne Young, and Shonda Blocker at First Baptist Church of Lincoln Gardens.

Contents

Introduction **11**
1 Some Things Never Change **15**
2 Building the Family **29**
3 Are You Really Listening? **39**
4 Mistaken Identity **47**
5 Communication Is the Key **63**
6 The Power of Forgiveness **75**
7 It Could Be Worse **87**
8 Real Love **101**

INTRODUCTION

A few years ago I spent three weeks in a rural community in Jamaica, West Indies. I was there to preach and I had decided to live with the people in this very poor, underdeveloped area. This experience changed my life. It was like being in America 150 years ago. There were no paved roads, only dirt. People lived in small houses without electricity. They had no running water in these homes, and the bathroom facilities were outside. The average family income in this district was $700 a year. I will never forget my visit with these people.

The most amazing part of my visit was my noticing how close these people were to each other and how strong their families were. At first I thought that no one could possibly be happy without cars, televisions, showers, stoves, and other modern conveniences. But I quickly learned that people can actually be happier without many of the things we assume bring happiness. Never have I seen a stronger sense of community and family.

Early in my ministry with youth, I discovered that family issues are the main concern for almost all teenagers. I have been invited to speak on numerous issues—sex, missions, self-esteem, drugs and alcohol, faith—and in spite of my topic I always receive a letter, call, or question from a young person that relates to family life. I discovered that most of the speakers and authors who dealt with this topic aimed their presentations at parents. This is certainly important. My pastoral experience has really shown me that married couples need as much guidance as possible as they build their relationships. But I also think young people can benefit by hearing and reading about family life and its importance and possibilities.

So I started speaking to kids about family. The response was overwhelming. I never dreamed the need was as great as it was. In the summer of 1988 I spent an entire week at a youth conference in Arkansas and spoke on family issues the entire week. It was then that I was convinced that I should attempt to write a book for youth on this topic.

This is my first book. I must confess that my first approach to this book was quite unsuccessful. I think I had become so accustomed to writing for seminary professors that I was incapable of writing for youth. It certainly was a shock to learn that I could speak to more than a million kids with great ease but could not write one book for these same kids. To solve my problem I had to begin listening to tapes of myself speaking to youth, and then had to "speak the book" before writing the book. (Unfortunately, none of the family talks which I had given to youth were available on tape.) After completing all of this I finally delivered my manuscript to the publisher.

I also made the decision that a book should not attempt to solve problems. No book I have ever read has solved a problem for me. Rather, books assist us as we reflect upon ideas and our response to our reflection becomes the way we solve our problems. Therefore, I felt that a lengthy book describing the different approaches to and philosophies about famiy would be boring and would go unread. I chose to share with you stories that contribute to themes that I have learned are important for family life. I hope these few chapters will give you some fresh ideas about the family you may feel to be driving you crazy. Then my prayer is that you will take these ideas and do something specific about your role in your family.

1. Some Things Never Change

A woman said to me one day, "Rev. Soaries, would you please speak to my son?"

"Ma'am, what seems to be the problem?" I asked.

"Every Saturday night my son goes with his friends to the shopping mall, and he just stays there until it closes."

"Ma'am, specifically, what would you like me to say to your son? What bothers you about your son going to the shopping mall on Saturday nights?" I needed to know if she thought her son was on drugs or perhaps she thought he had friends who were a negative influence. "What is he doing that's wrong? Does he stay out late at night?"

"No, he comes home at a decent hour."

"Do you think he is a member of a gang?"

"No, I think his friends are good guys."

"What is that *really* bothers you about your son going to the shopping mall on Saturday night?"

She looked at me very curiously and paused to think about what I wanted to know. Then with a very perplexed look on her face, she said, "I'm not sure. There just has to be something wrong with my son hanging out at the shopping mall every Saturday night. Maybe it's just that when I was his age, I never went to the shopping mall to hang out on Saturday night."

I looked at her and respectfully said, "Ma'am, when you were your son's age, there were no shopping malls here!"

She was amazed. This woman didn't understand her son because she grew up in a completely different world.

I am certain that if I spoke to her son, he would have said that there's nothing wrong with going to a shopping mall on Saturday night. It was normal for him. His friends did it, his cousins did it, and there were hundreds of other kids at the mall every Saturday when he got there. So here was a teenage boy and his mother who were in different worlds and didn't realize it. Things have changed so much since your parents grew up that it's almost as if you live in different cultures.

Our Changing Culture

I had another experience with a teenage girl and her mother who seemed to argue all the time.

They came to me and explained their problem. Every night at 10, the 14-year-old girl left the house, walked around the corner, and bought something at the 7-Eleven convenience store. The fact that she did this was driving her mother crazy. The mother interpreted this habit as rebellious behavior. The girl thought it was normal behavior.

The mother said, "My daughter has no respect for me."

The daughter said, "My mother does not trust me."

The mother could not figure out why the daughter felt she did not trust her. The daughter could not figure out why the mother thought she was rebellious. It never occurred to the mother that her daughter had friends who left the house at 10 P.M. to buy potato chips or soda at the 7-Eleven store. However, it never occurred to the girl that her mother grew up at a time when kids had to be in the house by the time the street lights came on.

That's what my house was like. My father used to tell me, "Buster, be in the house by the time the street lights come on." Of course, the lights normally came on at 6 or 7 in the evening because the sun was going down and people needed light to drive and walk without any difficulty. But even if the street lights came on at 2 in the afternoon, I had to be in the house. No doubt my sons will be like this teenage girl who knows nothing about the days when kids had to be in the house by the time the street lights came on.

So here were a mother and daughter who loved each other. (They both admitted that when they first came to see me.) But they were driving each other crazy, not because they didn't love each other but because they didn't realize how different they were and that they had grown up in different worlds.

Perhaps there are things about you and your parents that are very different and difficult. This situation may not be because your parents don't love you and certainly not because you don't love your parents. Rather, it is largely due to the fact that culture has changed so drastically between the time your parents grew up and the time in which you are growing up.

Let me give another example. When my family first got a television, my dad brought home a big, brown, cardboard box. He came into the living room, opened up the box, plugged the television into the wall outlet, and turned on the set. When the power was turned on, we looked at the TV with great excitement and anticipation. But when we looked at the screen, all we saw was a dot—a small, round, white dot in the middle of a large, grey screen. That dot was so exciting because it was the first evidence that we had a TV.

So we sat and watched that dot. While we watched it, the sound of a program began to originate from the back of the set. We could hear the voices of the people who were performing on the show. While we watched the dot and listened to the voices, the dot slowly s-p-r-e-a-d throughout the screen. After a few minutes, we could see the faces of the people whose voices we heard, and the dot turned into a picture. We finally had television. If you had that kind of TV today and wanted to watch a show at 8, you would have to turn the set on at 7:30 and wait for it to warm up.

Things have changed so drastically. Television itself is completely different. No more waiting for dots. As a matter of fact, you can turn it on and have an instant picture. Rarely does one see black-and-white TV anymore; we all watch color. Not only do we have color, but we have remote control. You can sit on your couch and change the stations.

When my little sister was in high school, I visited her at my mother's house. There she was, watching channel 2, taping channel 4 on the VCR, listening to a headset, talking on the telephone, and doing her homework all at the same time! I was alarmed that she was watching one channel and taping another. (There was no such thing as a VCR when I was her age.) I was incensed by the fact that she was listening to music on a headset at the same time. I was absolutely stunned by the thought that she was talking to a friend on the phone while doing it. What made me completely irate was the fact that she was changing channels with a remote control.

I said to my sister, "Terri, the least you can do is watch one program at a time." Every ten seconds, it seemed, she was changing the station from one to another.

She looked back at me and said, "Oh, you're just angry because when you were young and watched TV, all you had was a dot!"

She reminded me that things had changed so much that perhaps I had become angry at her for having things that I never dreamed about when I was her age. It is so incredible that most of us who are adults today have great difficulty accepting how different things actually are.

When I was a kid in school, for example, the U.S. government decided it had to keep up with the Soviets and others who were exploring space. The National Aeronautic and Space Administration (NASA) sent a spaceship into outer space with a monkey on board. I don't remember the monkey's name, but what I do remember is that the whole country prayed for that monkey. We wanted desperately for it to travel to outer space and come back safely. We were convinced that the future of America depended upon the safe return of this monkey.

Today, the space shuttle takes off, penetrates the atmosphere, and circles the globe. Astronauts wake up dancing to soul music and they stay out there for days at a time. The space shuttle comes back into the atmosphere, lands on an airstrip, and no one seems to notice. Yours is the first generation for whom that's true. We've gone, in just a few years, from praying every time a spaceship leaves earth to accepting it as a normal occurrence of life.

Your generation experiences as normal so many

things that every generation prior to now would have considered miraculous or supernatural. Just consider the computer. When we adults were kids, typewriters were the machines to learn. Today, second and third graders understand computers. A teenager can go to a store, purchase a personal computer and modem for a few hundred dollars, take it home to his bedroom, plug it into his telephone line, and call up computers around the world.

Yours is the first generation that considers heart and other organ transplants as normal. When I was a kid, a child with a bad heart lived as long as he could, then died. But today, there are hundreds of people waiting for new hearts, new livers, new kidneys. They are waiting for other people to donate their organs and for doctors to perform surgery. These procedures are all new.

But parents today often fail to recognize how different the world is. Perhaps this is why their own kids are not as excited about the same things that excited them, or not as interested in the same things that interested them, or not as inspired by the same things that inspired them.

God's Unchanging Designs

One of the wonderful aspects of Christianity and knowing God is that in the midst of an ever changing world, there are some things that just don't change. The things that do change are those that humans control. For example, humans control technology, fashion, and music. Therefore, all of the fast changes that occur in a society, and the world are those areas which humans control. However, if we continue to look at what has and has not changed, and if we are honest with ourselves, there are some things that just don't change.

Grass is still green. The sky is still blue. The sun, 93 million miles from the earth, still continues to shine. The earth rotates on its axis. Fish swim in water. Water still is two parts hydrogen and one part oxygen. Babies are born, and people die. These things never change.

When we consider the difference between the things that do change and the things that don't, life is brought clearly into focus. It becomes obvious that God intended that some things never change. When God created humans, He created them in some very specific ways. Most of those ways are obvious. God created male and female; that's obvious. Thus we have an easy way to distinguish between whether or not God made a man or a woman. God made different races of people, people with different hair textures, people with different skin colors, and people with different cultures. These things are self-evident. One can identify these differences in characteristics by looking and interacting with people.

But there are some decisions God made which are not as obvious. Chief among those characteristics is the idea that God made humans in His own image. That doesn't seem to be very obvious to people. It's not something you can see with your eye or touch with your hand. But it does suggest that God had something very specific in mind when He made humans. And it implies that God expected humans to share some of the attributes, or personality traits, that God has Himself.

The Family's Importance

Another less obvious characteristic that God gave humans is the idea that He intended us to live in groups. God did not make us like trees that grow independently. Rather, He made us in such a way that our growth, happiness, and successes are dependent upon our relationships with other people.

Those relationships are epitomized in what we now call family. Our family lives, our family units, our family relationships represent the greatest possibilities for human interaction and the greatest resources for human growth.

The first institution, the first organization, the first society, the first nation began as a family. That family was God's plan for guaranteeing the success for human development. It's no wonder that families have so many challenges. It is the most important unit or group or team that a person can have.

There is no substitute for a family. There is no replacement for a family; and, therefore, there is nothing more important to save and to build than our families. In the midst of a world that seems to be changing every day, the roles and importance of our families is something that never changes. It is true for people of every race, and it has always been true for people in every period of history.

I was reading once about Noah. I had always been impressed by Noah because he built a great ark. It had never rained before, which meant that to build an ark to protect anyone from rain required great faith. In fact, it was Noah's faith that impressed me for a long time. Then I was also impressed because God told Noah how many cubits high and wide and deep the ark should be. I noticed that Noah never asked God, "What's a cubit?" That impressed me because it was clear that Noah had an education and he at least had passed the course in cubits.

But what really impressed me about Noah was his response when God told him to include his family in the ark. There is no suggestion that Noah's family was religious, or righteous, or worthy of being saved. However, we do know that Noah was a righteous man; that is why God chose him to build the ark. We see this righteous Noah and a potentially unrighteous family. Yet Noah was close enough to his family to be able to find them and convince them to come with him on his ark.

I was riding in an airplane one day and thinking about Noah. I thought to myself, *Suppose God had called me, as He called Noah, to build an ark. And then suppose God told me that He wanted me to get my entire family and invite them to go on the ark. Could I do it?* Of course, I could find my mother; I know where she is. I could find my sister and brother. But suppose God told me to bring my entire family—my cousins, my aunts, all of those people who are considered a part of my extended family. Could I do it?

I took out a pen and a pad and began to write down all the names of the members of my family. In my community, we consider cousins and aunts a part of our immediate family, even though sociologists call them the extended family. I know people whom I grew up believing were members of my family to whom I was not related by blood at all. But I wanted to make a list of all the people who were, in fact, members of my immediate/extended family.

I wrote down all of my mother's sisters and brothers. There were eight of them, including my mother—four boys and four girls. Then I wrote down the names of all of my father's sisters and brothers. There were six of them altogether, four boys and two girls, including my father. My grandparents were all deceased. My father had also died.

I went from that list to the names of all the children of my mother's sisters and brothers and my father's sisters and brothers, who were obviously my cousins. What I noticed quickly was that I could not even *name* all of my cousins! It took effort. Finally, I did manage to remember all of the names of my cousins. But because we are no longer children, many of my cousins were married and had children. After recognizing that fact, I sought to list the names of my cousin's spouses and children. I failed.

I went back to the names of my aunts and uncles and cousins, those persons who had been close to me all my life. I attempted to identify where they lived. I failed. It became quite evident that although I frequently traveled to cities and states and nations around the world, I had failed to stay in touch with my own family.

As embarrassing as it is to admit, I went a long time without speaking a single word to my own brother. My first response to this discovery was to feel that I was justified in keeping my distance because my family drove me crazy. Well, not everybody in my family. But there were certain people that were easier to relate to than others. What I was really saying was that there were certain people in my family who were more like me than others. But I was quite embarrassed when I considered the fact that I was supposed to be a popular preacher who cared about kids and other people. I travel to tell people good news and apparently did not care enough about my own family to even stay in touch.

If I had been Noah and God had called me to build an ark and told me to save my family, including my cousins, I would have failed. That wasn't a good feeling. When I talk about family in this book, I will not emphasize cousins. But I've met people who live in the same house with others—parents, stepparents, children, stepchildren—who would fail, too, because they don't know enough about one another to truly call themselves a family.

I am convinced that although everything seems to be changing, God really intended for us to take families seriously. Even kids have a responsibility to keep families strong and healthy. And that's what this book is all about. Are you ready for the challenge?

Family Focus

1. Misunderstanding between parents and teens is not a recent occurrence. Even Jesus and His parents struggled with this problem. Read about it in the following passage:

> Every year His parents went to Jerusalem for the Feast of the Passover. When He was twelve years old, they went up to the Feast, according to the custom. After the Feast was over, while His parents were returning home, the boy Jesus stayed behind in Jerusalem, but they were unaware of it. Thinking He was in their company, they traveled on for a day. Then they began looking for Him among their relatives and friends. When they did not find Him, they went back to Jerusalem to look for Him. After three days they found Him in the temple courts, sitting among the teachers, listening to them and asking them questions. Everyone who heard Him was amazed at His understanding and His an-

swers. When His parents saw Him, they were astonished. His mother said to Him, "Son, why have You treated us like this? Your father and I have been anxiously searching for You."

"Why were you searching for Me?" He asked. "Didn't you know I had to be in My Father's house?" But they did not understand what He was saying to them.

Then He went down to Nazareth with them and was obedient to them (Luke 2:41-51).

What misunderstandings did Jesus and His parents experience? Why?

2. What are three or four activities about which you and your parent(s) disagree? Which ones may be due to the fact that culture has changed since your parent(s) were in their teens?

3. What activities did your parent(s) enjoy when they were your age? If you don't know, ask them.

4. Why is your family important to you?

5. Describe your family in three or four sentences. What aspects would you like to see improved?

2. Building the Family

When my wife told me she was pregnant, we were very excited. We had waited so long to have children, and it appeared that we couldn't have any. Finally, after four years of marriage, we were going to become parents. When we first got married, we could not financially afford to have children. Therefore, because we had waited so long and wanted children very badly, I immediately began praying that we would have twins. I thought it would be fair compensation for having to wait. Besides, my wife had a twin brother and none of her sisters who had children had twins. Therefore, I thought it was very likely and logical that she could and would have twins.

When Donna discovered I was praying for twins and asking people across the country to pray for twins, she began praying for me. But on November 1, 1989, Malcolm and Martin Soaries were born—identical twins. These boys have been the joy of our lives and a great challenge for both of us. The thrill of having twins never represented a great challenge to me, of course, until they were born.

One of the most important things we have had to do is find baby-sitters who are very dependable and competent. Not all baby-sitters are good with twins. But some friends and young people from our church have been very helpful. One of the wonderful baby-sitters we have been able to secure is a pre-med student who, when I met her, exuded enthusiasm, intelligence, and joy. She is a pleasure to know and a great help with the boys.

After my first meeting with her, I told Donna I had met a potential baby-sitter. What impressed me about this young lady was her level of seriousness, her self-confidence, and the way she carried herself generally. I said to Donna, "She must come from a good family." That's kind of an old-fashioned statement.

The Importance of Family

There was a time when people assumed something about your family if you acted or spoke a certain way. There are many people who still make those kinds of assumptions, either consciously or unconsciously. Most middle-class families that I know are not necessarily families with a lot of money but ones that subscribe to a certain value system. The role that the family plays in the transmission of these values and the perpetuation of certain cultural standards makes family life so important.

We have since learned that our babysitter does come from a great family. That didn't have to be true. There are so many wonderful, successful, stable individuals who come from very fractured and unhappy families. And there are many others who come from very stable families who end up having difficult lives with many ups and downs. It is true, however, that it is more likely that a person will be happy and well-adjusted if he or she is part of a family unit that is sincerely committed to mutual support and spiritual growth.

If you ever have an opportunity to visit a prison or study prison life, you will discover that the majority of the inmates share common characteristics. A lack of educational success is one. Another is the lack of a strong family background. A study was done in New Jersey a few years ago which indicated that the juveniles incarcerated in that state had in common—more than any other characteristic—the lack of parental involvement in their lives. This being true, I always encourage young people to insist upon the kind of family interaction they absolutely need but often lack.

Characteristics of a Good Family

What was it about my babysitter's family that caused me to conclude that she, in fact, did come from a good family?

First, her parents were educated people who held high standards for their family life. Education is very important for people's success in a complex, technological world.

Once I was attempting to travel from Seattle to Wenatchee, Washington. When I saw the size of the commuter plane, I became quite concerned that it was so small. What made me even more nervous was the fact that the same man who sold me my ticket was the man who checked my bags and carried them to the plane. Later, what made me extremely jittery was finding out that the same man was the pilot of the plane. When I realized that this young man was responsible for running the entire operation, my one concern was whether or not he was capable of flying the plane.

When we consider the importance of education, we must consider the fact that the world is so complex that it requires skills and abilities that were never important before. Education prepares us not only for positions that are crucial to the affairs of our society but also exposes us to great ideas, high standards, and various alternatives.

Family education is as crucial as individual education. It is great when families get together and learn how to do things, such as operating computers. It is a tremendous relationship builder when families fix plumbing leaks, mow grass, and paint walls together. There was a time when families were forced to do these kinds of activities together.

When I was a kid, we had to put coal in the furnace so the house would stay warm in the winter. Kids weren't allowed to go down into the coal bin alone. We always had to be accompanied by an adult. While we were scraping the old ashes out of the furnace and replacing them with new coals, we had unique opportunities to develop relationships with uncles, aunts, Mom and Dad. Technology has eliminated the need to go down in the basement and put coal in the furnace. Instead, we adjust the thermostat. However, no one develops meaningful relationships around thermostats!

My grandmother was a wonderful cook and my mother and her sisters used to gather in the kitchen to learn how to cook. But they also talked to my grandmother about everything. Now we cook our food in microwave ovens. It is hard to develop a relationship around a microwave oven when you just pop food in and it is ready in seconds or a few minutes.

The kind and amount of time people used to spend with each other is rarely repeated anymore. Today, we have to be creative and innovative to develop ways to cultivate relationships that used to be automatic.

For example, I know families who go camping together, who sing together, who attend church together, who go shopping together. Most families watch television together, but that is not really an activity that people do together. Granted, they sit in the same room; but they do not communicate and learn more about one another. Doing things together can be so important in building strong families. That's what impresses me about my baby-sitter's family.

The other thing I noticed about my baby-sitter's family is that they attempt to do things to meet each other's needs. We are a bit frustrated because she has another job working at a local appliance store that sells cameras, telephones, fax machines, and audio equipment. We have offered her more hours so she can quit that job, which she doesn't like. But she has one reason for keeping that job. Her dad wants to purchase a stereo component set. As long as she works at the store, she can buy his stereo at her significant employee discount. So until he saves enough money, she's going to hang in there and work at that store.

Naturally, we are disappointed that our baby-sitter doesn't have more time to spend helping us with the twins. But we admire this 19-year-old college student who is so committed to sharing her father's dream that she keeps a part-time job much longer than she wants it just to help him purchase his stereo.

Sometimes we call ourselves families when we act as if we are simply people who coincidentally live at the same address. We each have our own separate agenda, our own separate chores, and sometimes our own separate dreams. I believe there is no better person than a teenager to pull family efforts together and to create mutually cooperative activities. There is no question that activities like family devotions and special prayer requests can be effectively initiated by kids.

The interesting thing is my baby-sitter has never complained to us about her family. She has never described one problem nor has she ever criticized her parents in my presence. She probably does have some family problems. But she is one of the few teenagers I've ever met who does not have one complaint to share with *me* about her family.

She is accountable to very strict parents, but she appreciates the discipline they impose. That is the final thing that I recognize in her family. Her parents set very high standards for her. And she values those standards. She views them as evidence of her parents' love and concern for her.

She accepts the fact that if she is going to become a doctor, she has to be very successful academically. She accepts the fact that she has to work hard. She accepts the fact that she has to make sacrifices. My baby-sitter's parents reinforce all those ideas, and she accepts their reinforcement.

There comes a time when kids must accept the fact that adults have done everything the kids are now doing. Simply by virtue of the fact that they've been here longer, adults have to know more about most things than kids do. My baby-sitter is so impressive because she has such high regard for her parents' opinions and loyalty to their trust.

It's interesting that my baby-sitter and her family are not religious people in a traditional sense. They are nice people, and they appear to be happy. But they're not devout churchgoers, although they're not anti-church. They do appreciate and believe in God. I only mention this fact to illustrate that going to church and participating in the rituals of religion are not always the automatic solution for a healthy family life.

Don't get me wrong. I am an absolute believer in worship, prayer, Bible study, church attendance, Sunday School, and all that goes along with being a strong Christian family. But these activities are no substitute for logical, commonsense family interaction and respect for the potential that strong family life has to make a significant difference in all of our lives.

I expect my baby-sitter to date and marry a young man who has a similar appreciation for family. No doubt they will have children whom they will raise in a similar fashion to the way they were raised. It is very unlikely that this string of strong family tradition and values will be broken since we often become the reflection of our family backgrounds and environments.

I hope that some of what my baby-sitter knows, and does, and believes will add to what Donna and I are attempting to give our sons; and she will reinforce the values we are attempting to model in our own family. Together, we're trying to build a healthy family.

Family Focus

1. How much time does your family spend together in an average week? What can you personally do to increase that time?

2. What characteristics do you think are most important for a healthy family? How does your list compare with the ones given in this chapter?

3. In his letter to the Christians in Ephesus, Paul included a passage that offers guidelines for a healthy family. As you read this passage, underline all the actions that should characterize a healthy family.

> Therefore each of you must put off falsehood and speak truthfully to his neighbor, for we are all members of one body. "In your anger do not sin": Do not let the sun go down while you are still angry, and do not give the devil a foothold. He who has been stealing must steal no longer, but must work, doing something useful with his own hands, that he may have something to share with those in need.
>
> Do not let any unwholesome talk come out of your mouths, but only what is helpful for building others up according to their needs, that it may benefit those who listen. And do

not grieve the Holy Spirit of God, with whom you were sealed for the day of redemption. Get rid of all bitterness, rage and anger, brawling and slander along with every form of malice. Be kind and compassionate to one another, forgiving each other, just as in Christ God forgave you.

Be imitators of God, therefore, as dearly loved children and live a life of love, just as Christ loved us and gave Himself up for us as a fragrant offering and sacrifice to God (Ephesians 4:25–5:2).

Now circle the characteristics on which you need to work. Which one will you start with?

4. In what practical, specific ways can you attempt to meet the needs of your family members?

3. Are You Really Listening?

We will never get to know one another if we don't really learn to listen to each other. I am certain this is not the first time you've heard this statement, nor will it be the last; but it must be said. There is a difference between listening and hearing.

The big problem I had in communicating with my parents was responding to things they asked me to do. My mother typically said, "Buster, empty the garbage."

I was watching television, talking on the phone, or reading a book, or doing nothing. But I always responded by saying, "OK." To not respond at all would have been rude and resulted in punishment. To jump up and run to the garbage can and carry it outside would have been absurd. So my response was, "OK."

One hour passed, two hours, three hours. My mother came back and said, "Buster, I told you to empty the garbage." My response was, "I heard you." That response suggested that hearing her was adequate to address her concern.

It was quite clear to my mother that I had heard her—meaning my ears had functioned adequately to receive the verbal message which proceeded from her mouth. She had no concern about my capacity to hear. The real issue was: Had I listened to her? If I had listened, as she defined listening, not only would I have said, "OK," but I also would have emptied the garbage.

Listening Is . . .

There's a verse in the Book of James that addresses this issue: "But be ye doers of the word, and not hearers only, deceiving your own selves" (James 1:22, KJV). This statement helps to explain the difference between listening and hearing. The major way we learn is by listening. The way we discover new things about people is through listening. The way we discover new things about ourselves is through listening. What do we do when we listen? First, we hear. Hearing is important because it means that there is some degree of concentration and focus on what's being said.

My Aunt Carrie had a hearing problem of sorts. Once we were both in the kitchen, and I asked her a question. She was sitting next to me at the table, and I had to repeat the question three or four times because she could not hear me. She sat there, within an arm's reach looking at me, but she could not hear me. Because she was up in age and we were very close, I was patient and continued to repeat my question. She finally answered, speaking with higher volume than normal.

The next day I was in the living room talking to my cousin, and we were speaking almost in a whisper. My aunt was in the kitchen, washing dishes. When I told my cousin something I had planned on doing, my aunt shouted to me from the kitchen, "You better not do that!"

I was shocked! Just the day before, she was sitting within an arm's length of me and couldn't hear anything I said. The next day, she was in another room, making noise, and heard every word I whispered. At first I was quite confused. Then I realized that the problem the day before had nothing to do with my aunt's hearing, which was not consistent. The truth is she was very uninterested in the question I asked at the kitchen table. She was preoccupied with something else and had not heard me.

I think that's what happens to us sometimes. We often don't really hear people; either because we're preoccupied, we can't focus on what they're saying, or we aren't concentrating on what they're telling us. For example, perhaps your parents have tried to tell you that they love you—not in words, but by some other means. And you have not paid attention. Perhaps your younger brother (or sister) has attempted to tell you he really admires you. Often that admiration is acted out in ways that drive you crazy, so you ignore him. Or perhaps a parent or someone else in your family reveals through abuse or insults that he or she has a problem. If you really hear and focus on what's being said, you may realize something about that family member's problem. Hearing requires some degree of commitment and focus on what the other person is communicating.

But listening is more than hearing. Listening is interpreting what we hear. In the case of a person who has a problem, we sometimes allow our feelings to block the interpretation. If we have a family member who is constantly in trouble, we're often so embarrassed by the trouble that we don't process the fact or interpret the fact that he or she needs our help.

My boys have a tendency to cry when nothing seems wrong. If I allow their noise to be a nuisance to me, then I will not interpret the fact that their crying means that there is really something wrong even though it appears otherwise.

But listening is more than hearing and interpreting what people say. It can also be measured by the extent to which we're willing to respond. In black churches, one can determine whether or not people are listening to a sermon by the extent to which they say, "Amen," "Preach it Brother," "Break it down," or "Tell the truth."

Likewise, we can often measure our willingness

and ability to listen by our response to what we hear. After discovering my dad really was an English teacher like he claimed and processing a day I had with him in school, I stopped meeting him at the door and demanding immediate responses to my inquiries. Perhaps, if you really listen to what's happening in your home among your family members, you will begin to react to them a little differently because listening involves a response.

Learning to Listen

Learning to listen is a challenging task because it involves discipline. Assuming we have the desire to listen, there are specific actions we can take to learn how to listen. For example, I used to watch silent movies and show them to teenagers. We've become so accustomed to hearing music and voices that it is often difficult to focus and concentrate on pictures only. But you would be surprised at how many things you can notice when there is no sound.

Conversely, it's also interesting to discover how much you can hear without a picture. I have found great difficulty listening to a cassette tape of someone talking. My mind has a tendency to wander; I frequently rewind the tape to be sure I understand everything.

Another method of improving listening skills is to deliberately listen to things in which you have little or no interest. It's easy to listen to music that you like, for example. But it's difficult to pay attention to music that you don't like and then analyze it. I spent a number of weeks listening to rap music, attempting to analyze it, even though I don't like it. But that activity helped me become a better listener and learn more about how people who like rap music think.

Also, take time to get to know and listen to people. Sometimes it's easier to listen to someone with whom you have no emotional ties. Therefore, you may want to try listening actively to your manager at your job, the coach of your team, or a teacher before tackling immediate family members. If you think it would be embarrassing or difficult to sit with your father and say, "Dad, I don't really know you. Tell me something about yourself," practice on someone else first. But don't ignore your family members. You probably have elderly relatives who love to talk about their childhood and enjoy talking to young people. Take time to really listen to them.

Learning to listen is a result of a real commitment. It is not an easy activity, but it is worth the effort. A good listener is someone who will be successful and who will be able to build strong family relationships.

Family Focus

1. Read the following verses to find out what they teach about listening:

> Let the wise listen and add to their learning, and let the discerning get guidance (Proverbs 1:5).
>
> The way of a fool seems right to him, but a wise man listens to advice (Proverbs 12:15).
>
> He who answers before listening—that is his folly and his shame (Proverbs 18:13).
>
> My sheep [Jesus' followers] listen to My voice; I know them, and they follow Me (John 10:27).
>
> My dear brothers, take note of this: Everyone should be quick to listen, slow to speak and slow to become angry (James 1:19).

2. Define listening in your own words.

3. What specific methods can you add to the suggestions in this chapter for developing listening skills?

4. With whom can you practice your listening skills? When will you start?

4. Mistaken Identity

When I was a teenager, I thought my parents did not really go to work. I was absolutely convinced that my mother and father left every morning, appearing to go to a job; but in fact, they went to a meeting or a convention with other parents. At this daily convention, I was sure they sat around and discussed new ideas about how to make my life and other kids' lives unhappy. They then came home very excited about what they had learned. They took out their notes and tried new strategies on us.

One day when my father came home from work (at least he said he had been at work), I met him at the door. I greeted him with great enthusiasm. He immediately sensed that something was wrong. Never before had I been a one-person welcoming committee for him when he came home from work. I grabbed his bag and said, "Welcome home, Daddy."

He looked at me with great suspicion and asked, "What do you want?"

After telling him I didn't want anything, I quickly proceeded to tell him what I wanted. "Daddy, Joe is having a party Saturday night; and I would like to know if I can go."

He looked back at me and said, "Buster, I just got in from work."

Of course I knew that he had really been at a meeting with all those other parents, but I went along with the "work" story.

Then he said, "Let me go upstairs and take off my coat, read my mail, and get some rest. We will talk about it later."

"Daddy, I'm on my way to the park. All my friends are there. Everyone else knows who's going and who's not going; and when I get there, I'll need to tell people whether or not I can go to this party. So Daddy, I need to know now. Can I go to Joe's party on Saturday night?"

My dad looked at me. "Buster, I just walked in the door. I don't want to talk about this right now."

I thought, *What is wrong with this man? Was he born old or something? Wasn't he ever a teenager needing to know whether or not he could attend a party on Saturday night before Saturday night? Doesn't he realize we have plans to make? We've got to determine who's going to drive and what time we are leaving. I have to begin planning what I'm going to wear and decide if I need something new.*

As I looked back at him, I said, "Daddy, I need to know *now!* The party is Saturday night, and my friends know whether or not they are going. It's absolutely urgent! I must know: Can I go to Joe's party or not? I've got to know now!"

He calmly said, "Buster, if you need to know now, the answer is no."

"Dad, why don't you go upstairs, take off your shoes, read your mail, and take a nap. We'll talk about it after dinner." I couldn't believe my father didn't understand my immediate need to know whether or not I could attend the party.

I also could not understand why every day when he came home from "work" he insisted on going upstairs and taking a nap as soon as he walked through the door. What could he have been doing all day to require him taking a nap and getting so much rest? Then one day my school was closed because of a holiday. My father had told me that he was an English teacher at a junior high school in Newark, New Jersey. We lived in Montclair, approximately fifteen miles from Newark. The schools in Newark were open that particular day, so my dad invited me to go to school with him.

I thought, *This is a great opportunity for me to see where my father goes every day. He says he goes to work, but deep down inside I believe he attends a meeting with other parents. Now I will know what happens at these meetings!* So I quickly told him I was willing to go with him to school to see what he did at his "work."

We arrived in Newark early that morning. I discovered my dad actually did have a job and went to work at a school. My dad's English classroom was on the second floor. I went and sat in the back row. The first group of approximately 30 students entered the classroom.

I watched my dad as he attempted to teach those students English. They wrote notes to one another, they threw pencils at each other, and they asked questions without raising their hands. They laughed when things were not funny; and once in a while, they paid attention to the lesson my father was trying to teach. I had never experienced anything like this before in my life. The students in the school that I attended were much different than these. I never knew kids did these kinds of things in school.

The bell rang, and I watched another group of 45 students come into the room. I could not believe there were so many kids in one class. There were only 15 or 20 in my classes in Montclair. Again, I watched my father attempt to spend the next hour convincing these students that English was an important and interesting subject. He wasn't making much headway or having much success. The bell rang, and a third group of equal size entered. I watched a repeat performance.

After the third class, it was time for lunch. I joined my dad in the teacher's cafeteria. We quickly ate sandwiches. Then his job was to patrol the student cafeteria. He broke up a fight when a student tried to jump ahead of another in the lunch line. Students were throwing milk cartons at one another. I wasn't certain, but this seemed to be an unusually difficult day. After lunch, we went back upstairs; and I watched my dad attempt to teach two more classes. By the end of the day, *I* was exhausted.

I really hadn't done anything except watch my dad attempt to do his work. But doing so made me exhausted. As soon as we walked through the front door at home, Dad said, "I would like to talk to you about something."

"Dad, not right now. Let me go upstairs and take a nap. We'll talk about it after dinner."

That experience at my father's school gave me insight about him that I never had before. It never occurred to me that when he came home from work he was so tired that he took a nap not to avoid talking with me but to recover from a hard day's work.

Mistake Number One: Assuming Knowledge

An important question to answer is: Do you *really* know your parents? Do you really understand the pressures of their jobs, the difficulties they have financially, or even the physical limitations they have? I had made assumptions without really knowing my dad. There may be times when you want or need something from your parents, and their response is not acceptable to you. What do you do when your parents seem to be thinking on one level and you're existing on another? It's almost as if you find yourselves speaking to your parents on FM, and they are listening to you on AM.

So many of the teens I've met have made the mistake of assuming that they know their parents so well that they have them all figured out. That was the case with me. I thought I knew my dad so well that I could anticipate his every step. The cure for my problem was for me to spend time with Dad so I could get to learn who he was.

Perhaps your parents are people you don't really know. Have you ever been to work with them? It may not be a solution for everyone, but it sure worked for me. Perhaps there is another part of your parents' lives that you know nothing about and knowing more would help you understand them better. Of course, parents don't always want their teens poking into their personal business. However, most parents are impressed when their kids are willing to invest time and effort to get a better understanding about what they do and who they are.

It is to your advantage to have an accurate picture in your mind as to what your parents do during the day. What kind of stress are they experiencing? Is the company for which one of your parents works in a difficult financial period? Is the school where your mother teaches one with many problem students? Even if your mother stays at home, pressures such as bills, problems with the house, or even problems with the landlord may be causing her to respond the way she does. Just as we are affected by things that happen to us during the day, parents are affected in similar ways. Sometimes when they respond to us in ways we *think* we understand, we would understand better if we knew more about their daily lives.

Parents are human and people who need to be supported emotionally. They need someone to be proud of them as much as kids do. Parents also need support, motivation, compliments, and understanding. These are actions we usually expect from our parents, but where will parents get them if not from their own children? If you are committed to the idea that family is important, take the initiative to get to know your parents as well as possible. Don't make the mistake of thinking you know who your parents are or why they act the way they do without taking time to get better acquainted.

Not only is it important to know who our parents are today, but it is also important to know about their past—how life was when they were growing up. Chapter 1 highlighted the fact that culture has changed significantly. I found it enlightening to listen to my parents talk about their brothers and sisters gathering around the radio to listen to programs like "Dark Shadows." I could not believe a radio program would be so fascinating that people would sit around the radio the way we sit in front of television sets. But when my parents were growing up, they had no television. Many of the stories they know and the characters they admired were radio personalities. Finding out this information certainly didn't solve all of the problems that existed between my parents and me. But it did help me know more about who they were.

Mistake Number Two: Not Caring

The second mistake we often make in relation to parents is to assume that it is not important to know who they are. The issue is not that we think we know so much about them that we are experts, but rather that we don't really care to know. How could we not care? First, our parents—or the people who raised us—know us better than anyone else in the world. They changed our diapers, fed us bottles before we could even speak, and made a great emotional investment in us. The least we can do is to get to know who these people are, even in cases where our parents are not great (at least in our minds).

As a matter of fact, doing so may be especially crucial when parents are bad parents or even abusive. You probably know already that most reliable research suggests that parents who do their jobs poorly had bad parents themselves. It could be that you will be the person to help your parents seek the help they need once you discover the kind of childhood they had. The same can be true for someone who is living with a foster parent, an adopted parent, or a stepparent.

You can learn about a parent's childhood and past in ways that do not make you look like a private investigator. Games with personal questions can stimulate people to discuss their past. Or a class project may give you an opportunity to interview them or at least ask questions in an honest and innocent way. Talking with other adults who knew your mother or father as a child or teenager can give you a glimpse into his or her past. Remember, the goal is to discover something that will help your relationship and not to simply probe for the sake of probing.

One of your parents may have a secret problem or a problem they may think is a secret. I receive letters every week from teenagers who ask me for advice because their parents are drug addicts or alcoholics. They care desperately about their parents but don't know what to do. These kids have at least taken the time to recognize that their parents have a problem. Many of them discover that their grandparents had similar problems. Because of exposure to a negative environment as kids, these parents have become people with problems as adults.

You may live in a situation that requires the assistance of someone else. Before contacting anyone about your parent's apparent problem, make sure you have tried everything you can to discuss the situation with your parents first. If you feel you must talk with someone else, make sure this person can be trusted and will be respected by the parent with the problem. Since this situation is a very sensitive one, you would do well to ask for help from your minister or another professional who is close to you and your family.

No one plans to have problems. No one plans to fail. We often end up as the adults we are because of the environments in which we were raised as kids. One way to protect yourself from being the kind of adult you don't want to be is to get to know your parents so well that you discover how they became the kind of adults they are. This is of great importance when you have parents who are suffering, are abusive, or parent poorly.

Mistake Number Three: Giving Up

I also find that many young people assume that their situations can't change. They say, "My parents are driving me crazy, my family is driving me crazy, and there is nothing that can change that." This attitude prompts at least a million kids a year to leave home. They decide that whatever exists on the streets could not be as bad as what's happening at home.

Most parents want a good relationship with their kids, but few of them have been taught how to be parents. Sometimes it takes the kids to initiate the better relationship. *People can change.* Of course, people need to *want* to change; but people can change. When parents discover that kids have a genuine interest in who they are, how they became who they are, what factors affect their decisions, and other pertinent information, often they can be greatly affected and influenced by their teenagers.

I have discovered that many families who have family devotions do so upon the initiation of the kids. It's very difficult for a Christian mother or father to look a teenager in the eye and say, "No, I don't want to pray or study the Bible with you." *You* can make a major difference in your home. To think otherwise is to underestimate the amount of influence a child can have as a family member.

Although what I have written is addressed primarily to parent-teen relationships, the actions suggested also work with brothers, sisters, and cousins, particularly with stepbrothers and stepsisters. We are often forced to live in situations that we did not expect or desire. As a matter of fact, we don't create many of our situations. We can't choose who our are natural parents are, for example. Nor can we choose our natural brothers and sisters. We often feel we have even less of a choice when we are in blended families.

But, in fact, we have two choices. We can isolate ourselves from everyone else, decide what and who we want to be, and then become that person. Or we can invest time and energy to get to know people with whom we live. Sure, it is much easier to get to know someone whom we like. But even when we like someone, we often share only in those parts of their lives which we appreciate and ignore the others. The challenge is to really get involved in a person's life before deciding whether or not we like him or her. This does not mean we need to be nosy. It simply means we will wait to make decisions about people until we know what we are deciding on and who we are deciding about.

My wife traveled throughout Europe for six months before I met her, singing in a semiprofessional music production. While she was in Europe, she received a letter from her mother every day, even though the company with which she was working changed cities every three or four days. Although she was well into her twenties, she and her mother had the kind of relationship in which her mother wrote her a letter and she received a letter *every single day.*

Consequently, it was very difficult for my wife to understand how I could travel a lot and not call home frequently or write if I was away for several days. My initial response to this conflict was to think that she was possessive and insecure. But what I realized by getting to know my wife and listening to her experiences was that there was nothing wrong with her at all. Rather, she was the product of a relationship with her mother that gave her a particular perspective on life, travel, and family communications. This is an area that could have been a major problem if I didn't understand the kind of person my wife is and something about her background.

I share this illustration to reinforce the fact that any healthy, viable relationship begins with the people involved having a willngness and a desire to get to know one another. It is more than knowing someone's name or face or recognizing his voice. It involves an investment of time and energy to discover as much as you can about another individual even if the results of that discovery don't seem to be significant.

The family is the epitome of human relations. The way we maximize the strength of our families is to maximize the extent to which we really know one another. Based on this fact, how strong is *your* family?

Family Focus

1. How much do you know about your parent(s)' or guardian(s)' work day? About their childhood and teenage years? About their young adult years? How can you find out more?

2. Write a list of questions you would like to ask your parent(s) or guardian(s) in order to get to know them better.

3. In what ways would you like your parent(s) or guardian(s) to change? What can you do to initiate one or more of these changes? (Be sure to examine your own attitudes and actions in relation to these situations.)

4. Back in Old Testament days, a cupbearer (the person who tasted the king's wine to be sure it wasn't poisoned) named Nehemiah initiated a change in a relationship. Read about it in the passage below:

> In the month of Nisan in the twentieth year of King Artaxerxes, when wine was brought for him, I took the wine and gave it to the king. I had not been sad in his presence before; so the king asked me, "Why does your face look so sad when you are not ill? This can be nothing but sadness of heart."
>
> I was very much afraid, but I said to the king, "May the king live forever! Why should my face not look sad when the city where my fathers are buried lies in ruins, and its gates have been destroyed by fire?"
>
> The king said to me, "What is it you want?"
>
> Then I prayed to the God of heaven, and I answered the king, "If it pleases the king and if your servant has found favor in his sight, let him send me to the city in Judah where my fathers are buried so that I can rebuild it."
>
> Then the king, with the queen sitting beside him, asked me, "How long will your journey take, and when will you get back?" It pleased the king to send me; so I set a time.
>
> I also said to him, "If it pleases the king,

> may I have letters to the governors of Trans-Euphrates, so that they will provide me safe-conduct until I arrive in Judah? And may I have a letter to Asaph, keeper of the king's forest, so he will give me timber to make beams for the gates of the citadel by the temple and for the city wall and for the residence I will occupy?" And because the gracious hand of my God was upon me, the king granted my requests. So I went to the governors of Trans-Euphrates and gave them the king's letters. The king had also sent army officers and cavalry with me (Nehemiah 2:1-9).

What change in his relationship with the king did Nehemiah propose? Why? What strategy did he use? What was the result?

5. Communication Is the Key

Back in the Garden of Eden, Adam communicated very well with Eve and Eve with Adam. The problem was that their communication took them to the worst possible conclusion—sin.

Real Communication

Real communication is more than hearing. It also involves body language, emotions, understanding, and a desire for the other person's best interest. For example, people who fight are communicating; but their communication is destructive, certainly not in the other person's best interest.

God could have created us to be individuals, completely independent from other humans. Instead, He created us to need and desire the affection, attention, and nurturing of other people. All that occurs through some form of communication.

In the context of this book, we need to answer the question: Whose responsibility is family communication? I believe everyone is responsible. While parents have a major responsibility, teens have a share of the assignment also. Real communication takes commitment from all parties.

The hard part about this kind of commitment is the times when someone doesn't feel like talking. Mom and Dad, for instance, have a difficult day at work or are in the middle of a tough situation and want to be left alone. A teen flunks his history test or is stood up for a date and hides in her room. It is important to remember, however, that there is usually a part of a person that wants to talk or communicate even when things are difficult. After all, as humans, there's always a part of us that wants to be loved and nurtured by another human.

Promoting Communication

One way to let someone know you are interested in listening and sharing what he or she is going through is by saying something like, "I know you don't feel like talking," or "I know this is a difficult time for you to talk," or "You may want to be alone, but I just want you to know I care." Words like these communicate that you recognize the fact that he may have a burden or a problem and that you respect his right not to talk. But above all else, you want him to know that you are available to listen even if you can't do anything else. That message can be a very powerful way of communicating even without a lengthy conversation.

Another way to strengthen communication is by participating in the process. As I mentioned before, my mother often asked me to empty the garbage; and my response was "OK." Such one word responses to simple requests about household chores can hurt and hinder communication. I know it may sound silly and I may be exaggerating a bit, but imagine how much of a difference it would have made if the conversation had gone like this:

"Buster, empty the garbage."

Then I said, "Mother, I can promise you that I am definitely going to empty the garbage. I may not do it right this minute. But I can assure you, you won't have to remind me again."

We would have had to call an ambulance because my mother would have dropped dead from a heart attack! But at least I would have participated in this communication with my mom.

We seem to know how to communicate very well when we really want something, however. When we want money, we know exactly the right time, exactly the right way, and exactly the right tone of voice to make our request. When we want to go somewhere, we're very open to communication. I know that my father would often be very, very liberal in his giving up cash early in the evening. Morning was the wrong time to ask him; late at night was the wrong time to ask him. And so I had a strategy for asking for money, and it worked more often than not. But do we have a strategy for communicating with our parents in areas that don't relate to things we need? For example, I had a very embarrassing situation happen with my mom. I was in junior high school, and the most important thing in my life was to be cool. I needed to dress cool, walk cool, talk cool, think cool, eat cool. Being cool in those days meant that you wore certain clothes, had certain friends, listened to certain music, and went certain places. But being cool mostly meant that you had a certain attitude. Your disposition was cool. You never got extremely excited or overly depressed about anything. You were just cool!

My parents knew that I was dedicated to being cool; and in their own special way, they never made me feel stupid for trying to be cool. In spite of their apparent support, they weren't overly impressed with my attitudes and actions.

One day my mom got sick and had to go to the hospital. I can't remember what her exact condition was, but it was minor. I decided that I would express my love and concern for her by sending her flowers. I called the florist, made the arrangements, and stopped on the way home from school to pay for the flowers. They were delivered to my mother's hospital room.

When I went to visit her in the hospital that night, she was depressed and nervous. As a matter of fact, she had become very frightened about her condition. Immediately I wondered how she could have gone in for nothing serious and then, seemingly, taken a turn for the worst. What I discovered was quite embarrassing. It wasn't her condition that had made her feel worse. Rather, it was the flowers from me. She knew I was too cool to send flowers for a minor situation. So she assumed the doctor had told the family something very grave about her condition that she didn't know and that knowledge prompted me to send flowers. After all, what else could provoke this cool son of hers to buy flowers and tell his mother that he loved her? Then it hit me. I had never really told my mother that I loved her, other than signing my name to Mother's Day and birthday cards which my father usually bought.

Silence is a form of communication. What we don't say can communicate messages we may not want to give. I think we often perceive our parents as being responsible for starting discussions. After all, it's their job. But I often wonder if I could have been a better contributor to our family if I had worked more in the area of communication. Sure, I often asked questions about the Bible that I thought could stump my dad. Or I asked questions about my dad that I thought could stump my mom. But I think I missed opportunities to really contribute to the life of my family by not sharing my feelings.

I thought my parents were too busy to need to hear about how I felt about them. But what I have found to be true is that if kids really want to talk, most parents will make time to listen to what they have to say. It's really ironic. The problem most kids say they have is that they're lonely or bored. The problem parents most often tell me they have is that their kids won't express themselves, and they don't know how to talk with them. Both of these problems are easily solved if kids and their parents just begin speaking more with each other.

I once spoke at a family retreat for a church in Florida. This was my first experience speaking at such an event. Normally I spoke at either youth or adult retreats. But this church invited me to go with them to camp for a weekend and spend time with fifteen families. So there I was with moms, dads, and kids. There were some blended families—people who were divorced and remarried with kids from previous marriages. There were natural families (mom, dad, kids), and there were also a few single parent families. The purpose of this retreat was to help these families become better ones. I explained different Scripture passages, and told a lot of stories.

But what really made that retreat successful was the rain. Because it rained, all of the outdoor activities were canceled. Consequently, people had to stay inside with each other. By the end of that weekend, families that had been in turmoil, weakened by circumstances, or at war with one another were stronger families than they had ever been before. It was as if God sent the rain to force those family members to spend intimate and quality time with one another. They didn't need me or another speaker. All they really needed was concentrated time with no televisions, radios, or busy schedules in order to communicate.

What would you and your family do if you were locked in a room for a weekend? What would you talk about? What kinds of games would you play? What kinds of stories would you tell? Perhaps that's what you need to do. Perhaps it should be your idea. What would you do with each other there that you would not do at home? We have to begin to simulate these situations and create opportunities to discover the answers to these questions if our families are going to be strong. Maybe you're the one who will make that happen in your family.

The Foundation for Communication

The assumption that I have made is that you do love your family and that the foundation and basis for family communication is that love. One of the most difficult words in our language to discuss is the word *love.* One of the reasons it is so hard to consider is that we use the word *love* in so many different ways: "I love ice cream." "I love horseback riding." "I love basketball." "I love my wife." I may even say, "I love my friend." Each time we use the word *love,* we use the same word; but it has different meanings.

The Greek language distinguishes between different types of love. In Greek, brotherly love is one word; and romantic love is a completely different word. The kind of love that God has for people and that godly people have for others is another kind of love altogether—*agape* love. It's important that we distinguish between the various kinds of love so that when we talk about love for family and parents, we can be precise.

I was very close to both of my grandmothers. My mother's mother lived in New Jersey, and my father's mother lived in New York. Both of them were extremely special people to me. When I speak, I often refer to my grandmothers. My father's father died before I was born so I never met him. But my mother's father lived with us for many years. I knew him very well. When I tell stories about my childhood, I often tell about things I did with one grandmother, both of my grandmothers, and even my aunts and uncles, cousins and friends. Recently I realized that I never tell stories about my grandfather. In fact, one could assume—based on hearing me speak—that I never knew my grandfather.

The truth is that I never tell stories about my grandfather because he was an alcoholic. I realize now that his alcoholism caused me to erase him from my memory. Although I preached the eulogy at his funeral, I never had anything to say about him in my public life. Finally, I was forced to ask myself, "Did you love your grandfather?" The truth is that I did love him. But it certainly wasn't the kind of love I had for my grandmother. I don't talk about him with fond memories. I didn't go places with him.

Perhaps when we think about the word *love,* particularly as it relates to family, we think mostly about the "touchy-feely" kind of love, the emotional and affectionate kind. But that's not always possible. On the one hand, love can be very expressive, jubilant, and emotive while on the other hand, it can be very real but somewhat expressionless. The love I felt for my mother had never been expressed quite the way it was when I sent her flowers at the hospital. But I did learn that there had to be some kind of balance between my natural personality and desire to be cool and my ability and willingness to express to my mother the kind of love I did have.

So the question becomes: Do we really love the people whom we say we love? If we do, then we will commit ourselves to communicating with them and sharing with them the truth about our love for them.

Are you ready for this commitment?

Family Focus

1. One at a time, pretend you are each member of your family. How much does each family member know about you from what and how you communicate?

2. How can you initiate or improve communication with each member of your family?

3. Plan a special night to improve communication in your family. Take out a sheet of paper, and record specific answers to the following questions.
   a. What will you serve for dinner?
   b. What activities will you do together?
   c. What topics will you talk about?

4. The best description of love is found in 1 Corinthians 13. Read it several times; then summarize what you learn about love from this chapter.

> If I speak in the tongues of men and of angels, but have not love, I am only a resounding gong or a clanging cymbal. If I have the gift of prophecy and can fathom all mysteries and all knowledge, and if I have a faith that can move mountains, but have not love, I am nothing. If I give all I possess to the poor and surrender my body to the flames, but have not love, I gain nothing.
>
> Love is patient, love is kind. It does not envy, it does not boast, it is not proud. It is not rude, it is not self-seeking, it is not easily angered, it keeps no record of wrongs. Love does not delight in evil but rejoices with the truth. It always protects, always trusts,

always hopes, always perseveres.

Love never fails. But where there are prophecies, they will cease; where there are tongues, they will be stilled; where there is knowledge, it will pass away. For we know in part and we prophesy in part, but when perfection comes, the imperfect disappears. When I was a child, I talked like a child, I thought like a child, I reasoned like a child. When I became a man, I put childish ways behind me. Now we see but a poor reflection as in a mirror; then we shall see face to face. Now I know in part; then I shall know fully, even as I am fully known.

And now these three remain: faith, hope and love. But the greatest of these is love.

6. The Power of Forgiveness

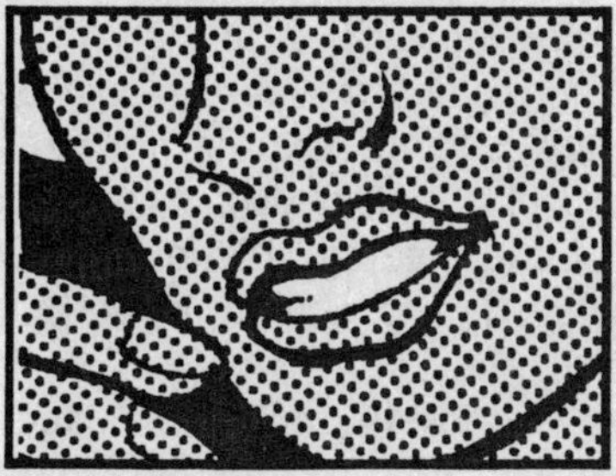

It was a beautiful afternoon in San Francisco. The sun was shining, the ships were by the wharf, people were busy shopping, and I had a few hours to kill. My friends had convinced me that since I had never visited Fisherman's Wharf, I should spend this pleasant afternoon browsing the stores and sight-seeing. I thought this was a good suggestion. So I joined two of my friends, and we boarded a bus to Fisherman's Wharf.

I was very pleasantly surprised by what I saw: wonderful shops, very friendly people, and great sights to see and things to do. While walking down the boardwalk, which was bordered by shops on the right and ships on the left, I noticed a large group of people lined up right in the middle. The line seemed to go nowhere.

I decided that since I had much more time to kill and since I am basically a curious person, I would investigate to see where this line was headed. So I took my place in line. I stood there and spoke to my friend who joined me. The line moved very slowly. Once or twice I got out to look to see where we were headed, but I could not see anything at the front. As a matter of fact, it appeared that the line just ended, going nowhere. As it got shorter and shorter, I was able to see what we were in line to do.

A teenager was seated on a milk crate, and people were lined up to sit next to him and have their friends take a picture of them. The reason these people wanted a picture with this teenager was due to the fact that he looked so strange. His head was completely bald around the sides, and his hair stood straight on its ends as a strip going from front to back. In addition to this Mohawk style, his hair was gathered into long spikes, each a different color. He looked weirder than anyone with that type of haircut I had ever seen before. He wore faded blue jeans with no shirt or shoes. After having their pictures taken, tourists handed this young man a dollar bill.

One Teen's Story

When my turn came, I sat down on the milk crate next to this young man, looked at him, and said, "I don't want to have my picture taken with you."

He looked back at me and very curiously asked,

"Well, then why are you sitting next to me?"

I told him I had seen people standing in line, had some time to kill, and decided to join them to see what was going on. But now that I was sitting next to him, I wanted to know what would make a young man, perhaps 15 or 16 years old, sit on the boardwalk at Fisherman's Wharf, allowing people to sit down next to him as if he were some kind of freak and take pictures for a dollar.

He looked back at me and responded that no one had asked him that question before. He had been doing this for a few weeks, and people had come and gone. But no one had stopped to ask him why he did what he did. He was very friendly, articulate, and willing to respond to my questions. He told me he needed the money to pay his rent. As I continued to talk with him, one guy in the line yelled, "Hey, buddy, hurry up!" But I wanted to find out more about this young man. So I told the people to wait a couple more minutes and I would be through.

I asked the young man why someone his age needed to present himself as some sort of freak or misfit in order to raise money to pay rent. He told me that he and his friend, another teenager, rented a room up on the hill in San Francisco. Both of them did the same thing to make enough money to pay their rent. Essentially, he had considered all of his options. He did not want to sell drugs or be a prostitute. So he decide that a legitimate way to make decent money would be to do what he was doing.

But my real question was why he needed to live on his own at his age. That's why I asked, "Where are your parents?"

He replied that his family lived in Ohio and he had been living on his own for two years. My next question was designed to determine why at 13 or 14 he had decided to leave home. I knew that more than a million kids every year run away from home; but he did not seem to be a bad kid, or a kid who was on drugs, or even a kid who had extremely urgent problems. I wondered what could have gone wrong in his life or his family to cause him to be one of those million kids.

He told me that his father had raped him. He went on to say that the father had promised he would do it again. And if he told anybody, he would kill him. The boy was convinced his father was very serious about what he had said and, therefore decided to run away. He came to San Francisco and met another teen who had run away from his father. The two of them decided that they would support each other in this manner.

I told this young man about people I knew in San Francisco who could help him establish a better life than the one he was living. I gave him the information, then walked away and let the next person in line have his picture taken with this young man.

I certainly didn't tell him he should go home and try to get to know his father better. He was a victim, and that is not the kind of advice I give victims. Sexual molestation and sexual violence seem to be a well-hidden but serious problem in today's world. I was recently in South Africa and was shocked at the number of white children who shared with me the fact that they had been sexually abused.

Seeking Help

It is important to know that when parents or other people are responsible for these types of acts, kids have a right to seek help. If this is happening to you, speak to your counselor, your pastor, a friend of the family, or even the police. Not only should you do so to protect yourself from further abuse; but you should also do so because the kind of behavior that results in abuse is the sign of a very serious spiritual, emotional, and psychological problem. Thus, in seeking help for yourself you may, in fact, be responsible for securing the kind of help your parent needs to address his or her problem.

By running away, the boy in San Francisco probably spared himself the trauma of another encounter with his dad. But he did nothing to address the problem his dad had. I heard a psychologist on a radio talk show tell a woman who had been raped by her father's friend that she had no responsibility for dealing with the feelings of the person who had raped her. In a sense, that could be very true.

Choice Number One: Forgiveness

But there are some people who accept this challenge that Jesus gave His disciples: "Love your enemies, do good to those who hate you, bless those who curse you, pray for those who mistreat you" (Luke 6:27-28). It's natural to respond to abusive people in a vindictive or spiteful, vengeful way. However, God wants us to pray for those who despitefully use us.

I am convinced the teen in San Francisco also has a tremendous challenge: Try to forgive his father for what he did. Forgiveness is one of the great keys to personal strength, mental health, and spiritual wholeness. As Jesus said, "If you forgive men when they sin against you, your heavenly Father will also forgive you" (Matthew 6:14).

I spent no time counseling this young man in the area of forgiveness, but I do believe that ultimately his ability to forgive his father will be a contribution to his own healing and victory in light of the circumstances. This concept becomes quite perplexing for those who really believe that an eye for an eye and a tooth for a tooth is the proper way we should direct our lives. However, Christianity offers us the most effective understanding of human wholeness and potential.

Choice Number Two: Hatred

Let's consider the boy's options if he rejects forgiveness. He could hate his father for the rest of his life. It takes time to hate; it takes thought to hate; it takes energy to hate; and hate uses emotional resources. Hatred is a logical response to acts of injustice which have been committed against someone. There are those who would tell the young man, "You're justified in hating your father." But let's consider for a moment the consequences of hatred:

- Hating his father will not change the fact that his father raped him.
- Hating his father will not change the fact that his father had a problem and needed help.
- Hating his father will never place him in a position to assist his father in receiving the help that he needs.
- Hating his father will take time and energy away from an alternative activity which could be directed to his own personal growth and development.

Hatred has its own way of breeding and feeding mistrust, fear, anxiety, tension, stress, and guilt. The feeling of hatred and the acceptance of that feeling can also turn into hateful activities that bring more harm to us than that which caused the hate in the first place. This young man certainly had just cause to hate. But hatred is not a productive response to pain.

Choice Number Three: Forgetting

Another choice the young man had was to attempt to forget about his father. But every day when he looks in the mirror, he'll see a reflection that resembles his father. There's something about the miracle of genes that causes us to carry a striking resemblance to people who are responsible for our lives.

For example, I look at myself every day; and, if I'm very honest, I see more and more traits of both my mother and my father. My mother is so beautiful, I've never minded people telling me that I look like her. And the more I confess that I look like my father, the more I realize that he wasn't such a bad-looking guy after all.

But if we attempt to totally wipe people from our minds, especially when those people are the ones responsible for our being here, we just cannot do it. I meet so many kids and receive so many letters from kids who don't know who their parents are; and that lack of knowledge is literally driving them crazy. Some of us, however, think we're going crazy because of what's going on in our families. But think of all of the people who feel as though there's something missing from their lives because they don't know who their mothers or fathers are.

This young man could travel the rest of his life throughout the world and never physically see his father again. But he would never be able to erase the fact of his father from his mind. If that memory remains only a painful and dreadful one, then he will be a victim of the abuse and the traumatic experience over and over and over.

The Choice of Champions

I recommend forgiveness because it gives us an opportunity to take the initiative in overcoming the pain and negativity of a bad experience. Forgiveness provides control, rather than forcing us to constantly revisit and relive the abuse suffered.

I had an experience when some guys tried to kill me. Since they were obviously unsuccessful, I've had to wrestle with my response to them. I discovered that when I allowed God to empower me to forgive them for what they did, I no longer had the problem of sleepless nights, angry feelings, fear, and frustration. Rather, I was able to live free of those results and look back to that experience as one that helped me grow. You may say that's easier said than done. Of course it is. Nothing as illogical as forgiving someone who hurt you is easy to do.

But God has promised to provide us with access to His power:

> I pray also that the eyes of your heart may be enlightened in order that you may know . . . His incomparably great power for us who believe. That power is like the working of His mighty strength, which He exerted in Christ when He raised Him from the dead and seated Him at His right hand in the heavenly realms (Ephesians 1:18-20).

God has promised that the power He used to raise Jesus from the dead is the same power we can use to be resurrected from the pain and misery of bad experiences, bad relationships, or bad memories. We certainly don't have the power in ourselves to forgive someone. That young man does not have the power to forgive his father.

But we do have the right to seek God. And God has promised that when we do seek His power, we will have access to it and not be left without the proper resources to do those things that would assist us in being healthy and whole people. When Jesus was about to be crucified, He literally asked God to forgive the crucifiers (Luke 23:34). Even before He went on trial, He washed the feet of Judas, His disciple, whom He knew would betray Him.

I am certain that something has happened in your relationship with your parents or stepparents, perhaps even your brothers or sisters, that gives you just cause to feel your rights have been violated. Hating them for what they did will not eliminate the fact that they did it. Attempting to erase them from your minds by not speaking to them, thinking about them, or talking about them, will not eliminate the fact of their presence in your life. Perhaps you should try taking charge of the situation by reducing the permanent effect that their treatment can have on you. Perhaps you can take charge first by forgiving them. Forgiveness doesn't cost anything, but it brings benefits that money can't buy.

Family Focus

1. What do you learn about forgiveness from the following verses?

Then Peter came to Jesus and asked, "Lord, how many times shall I forgive my brother when he sins against me? Up to seven times?" Jesus answered, "I tell you, not seven times, but seventy-seven times" (Matthew 18:21-22).

And when you stand praying, if you hold anything against anyone, forgive him, so that your Father in heaven may forgive you your sins (Mark 11:25).

Be kind and compassionate to one another, forgiving each other, just as in Christ God forgave you (Ephesians 4:32).

Bear with each other and forgive whatever grievances you may have against one another. Forgive as the Lord forgave you (Colossians 3:13).

2. According to these verses, what are the consequences of hating instead of forgiving?

Hatred stirs up dissension, but love covers over all wrongs (Proverbs 10:12)

Anyone who claims to be in the light but hates his brother is still in the darkness. Whoever loves his brother lives in the light,

> and there is nothing in him to make him stumble. But whoever hates his brother is in the darkness and walks around in the darkness; he does not know where he is going, because the darkness had blinded him (1 John 2:9-11).
>
> Anyone who hates his brother [continually] is a murderer, and you know that no murderer has eternal life in him (1 John 3:15).
>
> What other consequences can you add to these?

3. Has one of your family members hurt you? How have you responded? If you have not forgiven him or her, will you do so now?

7. It Could Be Worse

A woman in her mid-40s and her mother lived together. The older woman not only loved her daughter, but many family members accepted the fact that this was her favorite child and she would do anything possible for her. The younger woman had been divorced for a number of years and had one daughter herself.

One day the mother decided to go on a trip for a few days with two or three other family members. She prepared in advance with the daughter's help. The day to depart arrived. The mother, realizing that the daughter who was driving her was ready to leave, went outside.

While standing on the porch, she looked around but didn't see her favorite daughter. She went back inside the house to find her and say good-bye.

When she could not locate her, she decided to wait in the car.

When her daughter finally realized that her mother was ready to leave, she came running out of the house, slammed the door, and began cursing her. This daughter's anger was evidently provoked by the fact that she thought her mother was going to leave and not say good-bye to her. The daughter's cursing was so embarrassing and painful for the mother that all she could do was cry. She got out of the car and went back to the house to say good-bye to her angry daughter. As she approached the porch where her daughter was standing, the daughter ran into the house and slammed the door in her mother's face.

A few days later, the state police called the daughter's home about midnight. When she answered the phone, the officer reported that her mother had been killed in an auto accident. The daughter was physically, emotionally, and psychologically unable to handle the news. She had been a very strong, capable woman until that point. She had been employed as a health-care professional; but, after this experience, she was never able to work again.

I'm not a psychologist or psychiatrist, only an observer of this situation. However, I am absolutely convinced that something happened to this woman when she realized that the last scene in her relationship with her mother was her slamming the door in her mother's face after having cursed her in front of neighbors, relatives, and friends.

The Time Is Now

I have talked with so many people who don't take seriously the biblical admonition that we should not let the sun set on our anger (Ephesians 4:26). While many of our situations are not as intense as this woman's, we often fail to reconcile our differences in a timely manner. Perhaps you are much stronger than this woman and can handle the risk of tension and disagreement easily. But I suggest that when we do have squabbles with our parents or others, we should attempt to mend the relationships as quickly as possible. The famous excuses, "It's not my fault" or "I didn't start it," are not the point. If any relationship is worth having, it's also worth saving. I would hate to see anyone repeat what I've watched this woman go through. Her life has never been the same.

Attempting to heal the wound or resolve the tension doesn't always have to be done personally or physically. Perhaps you could send a card; there are cards available for almost every situation. Sometimes it's good to write a letter or make a cassette tape and mail it. Or use someone else's words. But when you've had an argument or disagreement with someone you love, particularly one of your parents, try not to let a day pass before attempting to reconcile with him or her.

It's not as easy as it sounds. It almost requires

that the other person also desires to reconcile since it's very difficult to make up with someone who doesn't want to. But often teens assume that it's the parents who need to take the first step or to forgive because it's their responsibility to take care of you. I think adults become much better parents and are much easier to deal with when teens take the initiative and say something like: "You know, I don't know what happened this afternoon. But things really got bad, and it bothers me when we fight. I'm sorry for what I said."

My sister has always been good at reconciling. Our dad died when she was 8 and I was 24. I assumed a semi-father role and attempted to assist my mother in raising my sister. That is a strange relationship—not quite father, not quite brother, a little bit of both. However, she has always been able to discern when there is some stress, tension, disappointment, or disagreement in our relationship. She often took the bite out of a situation by saying, "I feel really bad about what I did" or "I'm sorry for what I said" or "I'm sorry for what happened between us, and I don't want it to happen again." We've never had a major argument, primarily due to the fact that if something negative began to develop, she cut it off with that kind of conciliatory gesture. Therefore, I know what I'm suggesting works. It worked on me in spite of the fact that there were times when I looked forward to a good argument with my sister or someone else in my family.

I guess what I'm trying to say is that going crazy, staying crazy, and talking about being crazy is not the only option for family life. Family life can be fun; it can be interesting. It will never be the same every day, but it certainly can be more than we expect it to be. It's just not going to drop out of heaven and be all that we want it to be, however. It takes work; it takes time; it takes commitment; it takes a level of seriousness; and it takes God.

God created families, and God will have to be the one who keeps families together. I often think about my baby-sitter who doesn't depend on God to maintain a good family. I often say to myself and to her that if she can have such a wonderful life without God being the center, imagine how awesome it would be if the Creator of the Universe were to get involved.

It Could Be Worse

I was reading a story about Jesus, and it seemed to me that He did a dumb thing. A crippled man's friends brought him to Jesus because they thought He had the power to heal him. There was only one reason the man was sitting in front of Jesus—he needed to be able to walk. Jesus looked at this man and said, "Son, be of good cheer" (Matthew 9:2, KJV). Can you imagine Jesus saying those words? I couldn't figure that out: "Be of good cheer."

What He was actually saying was, "I know you can't walk; you'll never play football. You've never ridden a bicycle. When all the kids went ice skating, you had to stay home. But be of good cheer. You can't hold a job. You have to beg for a living; people give you the leftovers from their table because you can't work. But be of good cheer. You can't wear nice clothes. When it rains, you can't get up and go inside. You live totally dependent on the whims of other people. But be of good cheer." I could not figure out why Jesus told this man to be of good cheer. I could understand it if Jesus told him to be of good cheer after he was healed, but the man still had the problem when He spoke those words.

There are times when you may feel as though no one understands your problems. Everyone advises you to cheer up, to forgive your parents, to get to know your parents better. But deep down in your heart, what you're saying is, "There is no way possible you could know my situation. If I were this man who was sitting in front of Jesus, unable to walk, I probably would have said, 'Jesus, You heal me, and I *will* be of good cheer.' "

Sometimes religion and religious leaders have a tendency to oversimplify people's problems. Nothing is more frustrating for me than to hear preachers on the radio give people the impression that if they become Christians, all of their problems will be solved. Jesus, however, approached problems from a different perspective. While He clearly had the power to solve the man's problem—and later He did, He offered the man practical advice as to what he could do even while he had the problem.

There is no way humans can live with other humans and not have problems. Likewise, if the problem or challenge you may be experiencing with your family goes away today, there will be a new one tomorrow.

Jesus' idea of being of good cheer while you have a problem has become a source of great inspiration for me. Sometimes I believe He said that because the man could obviously hear and see, and he had a number of wonderful things happening in his life beyond the fact that he could not walk. Perhaps Jesus looked at this man and thought, *He's crippled but he's* only *crippled.* In other words, perhaps Jesus was saying to the man, "Cheer up; it could be worse."

I was traveling in Jamaica once. At the end of my trip, some people invited me to visit a facility where some very sick people were housed—young children who had been abandoned by their parents and old people who couldn't afford to go to the hospital. There were 400 sick people and 1 nurse to address all their needs.

The last person I saw was an old man with no legs and only one arm, sitting on a bed. I'm not always comfortable around very sick people. It sometimes feels as though there is nothing that I can say to comfort them. As I approached this man's bed, my plan was to smile at him but to keep walking. As I approached his bed, I smiled as I planned and said hello. As I attempted to walk past his bed, he reached out with his one arm and grabbed my wrist. It was clear that I had to stop to speak with him. What would I say? When I did stop, I didn't have to think of what to say to him because the man spoke to me.

"Young man, where are you from?"

"I'm from New York City."

Holding my wrist, he continued the conversation. Then he asked, "When are you going home?"

I told him I was flying home that same afternoon.

He held my wrist firmly with his hand, looked directly into my eyes, and said, "I'll be praying for you."

I stood there amazed. Here was a man who had no legs and one arm, who would be confined to a bed in this institution for the rest of his life. He had either little or no money, only a few friends, few opportunities to go anywhere or do anything. And here I was—physically fit, healthy, money in my pocket, American Express card (don't leave home without it), friends, family, and opportunities to fly around the world.

I thanked the man for what he said, then added, "Sir, there's something wrong here. I'm the one who should be praying for you."

He looked back at me, and I'll never forget what he said. Still holding my wrist with his one hand, he said, "Son, you've got two legs; I've got none. You've got two arms; I've got one. But you know what? *It could be worse.*"

Every time something bad happens to me, I

think about that old man with no legs and one arm. I reflect on the fact that he had some problems, but he recognized that they could have been much worse. As a result, he didn't feel crippled. We call him handicapped, but he considered himself blessed.

There are probably times when you feel that your problems can be no worse than they are. Or there may be times when you feel that your parents are more peculiar than any kid's parents on earth. Such thinking is a danger sign. When you think things cannot be worse, you try things that you know could be harmful to you. As a matter of fact, it's when you really believe that life cannot be any worse that you could even decide it is not worth living at all.

When I spoke at a conference in Minnesota, I met a girl who was having a very serious family problem. When I was through speaking, she came to me in tears and said, "Buster, we must talk." Both her parents were having serious difficulty with each other although this girl's home looked like a model Christian family from the outside. (That's one of the reasons I'm not always impressed by the fact that mom and dad and kids live at home together. There really are some single-parent homes that are happier.) As she talked, I remembered another terrible situation.

The family that came to mind was a mother and five children. I had become quite friendly with all of the children through my ministry in New Jersey.

One of the girls was literally a gangster by the time she was 14. But we became the best of friends. She allowed God to change her life, went on to complete college, and is now a successful junior executive at a New York City bank. But through that process, I had to encourage this young lady because of her family situation.

Her mother came home in the evening and was somewhat abusive toward her kids because she had been drinking. Sometimes she awakened her daughter, the one whom I was befriending, and forced her to wash dishes at 2 in the morning. When this girl was 15, I made an agreement with her that she could call me anytime she had a problem or needed to talk. She called me late at night in tears, wanting to run away, wanting to do something to her mother, sometimes even wanting to do something harmful to herself. I talked with her, prayed with her, and counseled her. I took her places with me and tried to help her grow spiritually and emotionally.

When she came to mind, I looked at the girl in Minnesota and told her to come to the phone booth with me. It was 3 in the morning, but I wanted her to talk to my friend in New York. I awakened my former juvenile delinquent friend from her sleep and told her there was a young lady standing by the phone who needed to talk with her. All I told her about the Minnesota teen was that she thought she had the worst family situation any kid could have. I wanted my New York friend to explain what she had encountered with her mom when she was a teenager and to tell her how she responded to her crisis.

By the time the girl from Minnesota finished talking to my New York friend, she was laughing and crying at the same time. She realized that, compared to my friend's, her situation was nothing at all. Therefore, she was laughing at herself for having felt it was as bad as it was. She was crying because she felt sorry for my friend, although she was doing well now.

One of the ways teens can help each other is to remind each other that family situations really could be worse. The fact that you're alive and reading this book means that life could be a lot worse. The fact that you can think about and reflect on things that have happened in your life means that it could be worse. The fact that you are able to connect with people who know something about God and can share with you the answer to life's greatest problems means life could be worse. Once I realized that situations could be worse, I was able to identify what was OK.

When it's dark outside, it's difficult to realize that the sun is shining somewhere else. When you have an argument with your mother, father, or someone very close to you, it's difficult to focus on positive aspects. I'm sure it was difficult for the crippled man to be grateful for the fact that he had eyes to see, ears to hear, or hands that worked OK. He focused on the fact that he could not walk, and that's understandable. But there are times when the absence of immediate solutions to our immediate problems suggests that we should spend time focusing on what we do have and not dwelling completely on things we don't have. Even relationships with our parents give us opportunities to consider the things that are good about them.

When I talk with my wife to check on our relationship and we spend time evaluating how aspects of it can be better, we always start with what we like about each other. Then we move on to aspects that possibly can improve. The fact that things could be worse means that there is something worth remembering and protecting.

It's Your Move

When was the last time you seriously made a list of all the wonderful things you know exist in your family? It could be quite interesting! It could be the step that starts you on the road to reconciliation. Perhaps it's something your whole family could do as an exercise. You may want to try calling a family meeting and have everyone write down on a piece of paper four or five things they love about other members of the family.

Don't wait for situations to get so bad that you can't talk about them or you feel they could not be any worse. Recognize that in the midst of the worst problem, it could be even worse and may in fact get better.

Family Focus

1. What do the following verses teach about reconciliation?

> Therefore, if you are offering your gift at the altar and there remember that your brother has something against you, leave your gift there in front of the altar. First go and be reconciled to your brother; then come and offer your gift (Matthew 5:23-24).

> "In your anger do not sin": Do not let the sun go down while you are still angry (Ephesians 4:26).

2. With whom do you need to reconcile? How will you do it? When?

3. What's your current problem with your parents or other family members? How could it be worse?

4. What's right with your family? Identify at least six aspects.

8. Real Love

So far we've examined a number of ways to improve family relationships. But the real issue is whether or not we truly love our families. To find out, we need to compare our love with the real thing. The best description of real love is found in Paul's first recorded letter to the Christians at Corinth. For Paul, love was the most important virtue a person could have. Let's look at what he wrote about love in 1 Corinthians 13:4-8a:

> Love is patient, love is kind. It does not envy, it does not boast, it is not proud. It is not rude, it is not self-seeking, it is not easily angered, it keeps no record of wrongs. Love does not delight in evil but rejoices with the truth. It always protects, always trusts,

always hopes, always perseveres. Love never fails.

Love Is Patient

Paul began by describing love as patient. What does it mean to be patient? Patience is knowing we deserve something but being willing to wait for it. Patience is knowing someone owes us something but gracefully waiting for him to deliver it. Patience is needing something immediately and—even if you don't receive it—waiting with a smile on your face.

Many of us say we love our parents, but we are not patient with them. We expect our parents to be patient with us, however. We want them to wait for us to take out the garbage. We want them to wait for us to become serious about our school work. We want them to wait for us to grow up and get a job so we can contribute to the family budget. We want them to wait for us to experiment with our various relationships. We want them to wait for us to get up in the morning.

But are we willing to be patient with our parents? Are we willing to wait and give them a chance to respond to our requests, or do we demand immediate answers? Are we willing to wait and give our parents an opportunity to save more money before purchasing things that we want, or do we want what we want when we want it? If we really love our parents, we will work very hard at being patient.

Love Is Kind

Paul wrote that love is kind. How kind are we to our parents? One of the complaints I often get from young people is that their parents say things about them in front of others that embarrass them. As a result, I have given numerous talks to parents, asking them to consider being sensitive to the feelings of their children and not embarrassing them, particularly in front of their friends.

The worst experience I ever had as a child was when my dad came to school for a surprise visit. I'll never forget it—I was in sixth grade. He came to school unannounced, just to check on how things were going. When he appeared in my class, my teacher was out of the room and I was attempting to entertain the class by standing on top of my desk, dancing, and telling jokes. My father caught me in the middle of my act and took me into the hallway. Needless to say, he communicated very effectively with me! For a long time I felt that was the cruelest thing my dad could have done to me. However, I did grow to appreciate the fact that he at least took me out of the classroom and did not attempt to embarrass me in front of my friends.

I can honestly say I wasn't that kind to him when I was a kid. Sometimes when we were in public, I wanted to know something from my dad immediately or felt I needed to say something important to him. I probably embarrassed him, or, at the very least, rudely interrupted him. I would never have wanted my dad to embarrass me the way I often embarrassed him.

I am certain we all do this occasionally. Even the way we dress deserves some attention. We often say, "I'm an individual; I have a right to dress any way I choose." But love suggests we are so willing to be kind that we consider what would make someone else happy even if it involves our personal attire. Often we wear certain clothing because we know it pleases a special person, but we can become a bit rebellious if our parents suggest they may like to see us in different attire. Love considers doing something purely for the benefit or enjoyment of someone else.

Love Does Not Envy

The next characteristic of love is lack of envy. This relates not only to our parents but also to our siblings. How often do we say, "You [parents] did it for him or her, why not for me?" Or, "She's able to do it; why can't I?" For example, my parents could stay up late at night and watch the Johnny Carson Show at 11:30. I thought it was cruel and unusual punishment that they could watch Johnny Carson and I had to go to bed. They always told me I had to get up the next morning to go to school, but I could not accept that reason. Obviously, however, I could not base what I was allowed to do upon what they did for themselves.

Envy is wanting something that someone else has. Whether that someone else is your mother or father, sister or brother, cousin or friend, love requires that you do not respond to a relationship based on what someone else has. If the only reason we want items or privileges is because someone else has them, then our tempers may flare when we are disappointed, risking ruptured relationships. Instead, if we love someone, we should be happy that person has what he does.

Love Does Not Boast

Boasting is a result of feeling that anything you have or you do is much more significant and important than anything someone else has or does. If we score two touchdowns or get an A on a test, we often want our achievement to be the center of attention. We want our accomplishments, or the way we look, or our new hairstyle, or our new friends, or our new cars to be the focus of all the discussion. We want the entire family to celebrate with us those items or achievements that represent our victories. But Paul wrote that when we love people, we do not project these into the spotlight of our family lives.

Love Is Not Proud

The next characteristic of love is related to boasting. God says, "Pride goes before destruction, a haughty spirit before a fall" (Proverbs 16:18). Pride, essentially, is the result of a person being totally self-centered. That is actually what causes someone to boast. Have you ever noticed that the word *pride* has the letter *i* right in the middle? Pride declares that *I* am more important than anyone or anything else at all times.

Everyone should have a healthy and appropriate amount of pride, thanking God for the wonderful gifts and achievements He has given them to enjoy. Pride becomes negative when we focus only on ourselves, ignore other people's gifts and needs and take all the credit for what we accomplish. (By the way, the word *sin* also has *i* in the middle. When we have ourselves as the focus of all our attention and we must be the center of everything, then we are both guilty of pride and prone to sin.)

Love Is Not Rude

There's a young man who lives across the street from my family. When his mother calls him for dinner, he responds with profanity and vulgarity. His response is an embarrassment to his family, I'm sure, because it is an embarrassment to our entire neighborhood. He certainly is the most rude young man I have ever met. It would be difficult for him to convince anyone that his rudeness is an expression of love.

Love Is Not Self-Seeking

Self-seeking goes back to being proud and boastful. But it also implies that the only things that interest us are those that relate to us. But love motivates us to be as interested in something that benefits another person as we are in something that benefits us. For instance, if my father is preparing to go on a business trip or to a social function, love prompts me to be as excited about his activity as I would like him to be about my receiving an award.

I remember the night of my high school graduation. I was very nervous and excited about being the student who would give a speech. Later, when I was an adult, my mother was completing her college education and was scheduled for a senior music recital. I was extremely busy at that time. My dad had died; and being the oldest son, my mother looked to me for support. While I love my mother, I could not get excited about her senior recital where she'd be singing German or French songs and other kinds of music that I neither understood nor liked. But I thought back to my high school days when I was excited and nervous about my graduation speech. I remembered that my mother had been as excited about my speech as I was. It was that memory that convinced me that if she could love me enough to be excited about my graduation speech, then I should in turn show her the same kind of love. We call that reciprocal love. That's what Paul meant when he said love is not self-seeking.

Love Is Not Easily Angered

It's easier to be angry at people whom we love than at people we don't love. It's the people who are close enough to us to make us angry who do so. These are the ones who disappoint us, who hurt us, who embarrass us, who humiliate us. The type of love Paul described here is the kind that prompts us to temper our temper. Consequently, we do not jump to conclusions or respond primarily based on what we have the right to do. Instead, we respond in love, knowing that even if a person is wrong, our primary response should not be anger.

Love Does Not Keep Records of Wrongdoing

I've never met a young person who does not insist that it is unfair to bring up things from the past to use against him. Parents seem to do this all the time. We might get reprimanded or punished for something. After the issue is supposed to be dead, our parents remind us about it again. Nothing hurts more than to be slapped with a mistake we made for which we have already been punished. We call that tactic "throwing it up in my face."

But we do the same thing to our parents. We keep a mental list of what they've done wrong to us. Then, sometimes in an effort to defend ourselves, we throw one back in their faces. Love, according to Paul, implies that we keep no record of the wrong things that people do to us.

People often say, "I can forgive but I can't forget." What Paul is describing here is the kind of love that says, "Not only will I forgive, but I will forget; and I'll never bring this up again." If you've ever been hurt or disappointed, if someone has done something to you that you know you did not deserve, it is very, very difficult to treat that person as if he never did it. But when we love a person, this is exactly what we strive to do. This biblical concept is the highest understanding of love known to humans.

Love Rejoices with the Truth, Not Evil

Furthermore, Paul wrote that love is not happy about bad things that happen to people. If we love someone, his pain is our pain, his disappointment is our disappointment, his grief is our grief even when he has done something wrong to us. Notice that this characteristic immediately follows the fact that love does not keep a record of wrongdoings. If we keep a record of the wrongs people do to us, then when something evil happens to them, we feel as though they deserve it. In that case, we will actually be happy.

But Paul said if we love someone, we can't delight in evil, we can't delight in problems that other people have, we can't rejoice, we can't be glad. We shouldn't be happy if something bad happens to someone else. This ideal is especially true and challenging with stepparents. If your mom is married to a man you don't necessarily like, it can be easy to want something bad to happen to him or between them because you perceive him as interrupting your life. But then you have to consider: How does your attitude make your mother feel? How does it make your stepfather feel? After all, he's human. You may not like things that he does. But if you love your mother and are attempting to be a loving person, then you have to learn how to love him even when you don't love what he does.

The real beauty of biblical love is that we are challenged to love everyone. Jesus taught us to love our enemies. That may not mean we love them with affectionate hugs and kisses. And it certainly doesn't mean that we love the fact that they are our enemies or that they attack us and attempt to do things to us. But we can learn to love people even if we hate the things they do. We can love the person without loving his deed. If we hate the person, then we will wish evil and harm on him. But if we love the person, we won't be happy when evil happens to him. Instead, we will delight and rejoice in the truth and the positive things that happen to him.

Love Protects

Love always protects. Isn't that one of the great responsibilities of love? Recently, I talked to a mother who has a teenage son in jail. He's been accused of a very terrible crime. If he's guilty, his mother will hate what he did for the rest of his life, but she knows jail is no place for a person his age to be.

She looked at me and said, "Rev. Soaries, my son may be guilty, but I want the best for him. If he's made a mistake, I want him helped, not just punished."

Love always protects. That doesn't mean we lie for people. It doesn't mean we ignore others' wrongs. But it does mean we try to protect people from the kind of things that can make bad matters worse or about which people may not be aware.

I was in Washington state traveling to a retreat. Ahead was a potentially dangerous situation on the road. Until the danger was cleared away, I took it upon myself to jump out of my vehicle and stop cars, making sure others were not victims of any tragedy that could have occurred on that highway. I was really compelled to do that based on my love for people. If you love people, even people you don't know, you don't want them to be the victims of some kind of tragedy from which they could have been protected.

In our families it's our responsibility to protect one another. It is even a teenager's responsibility to protect his parents from words people might say about them and to protect his family from actions people might do to them. Paul states that we have a protective responsibility. That's the kind of love God has for us.

Love Trusts

Love always trusts. That's a difficult action. It's particularly hard because we find it difficult to trust people in situations in which we are not sure they are trustworthy. If I were walking down the street and a German Shepherd trotted toward me, the first thing I would think of is to run for my life.

Therefore, if someone said to me, "Buster, walk down the street with me. If the German Shepherd comes, I'll protect you." I'd have difficulty trusting that person because I'm not sure he could keep his promise.

Where there is mutual love, then we know we have the kind of relationship that says we trust each other. One of the reasons I consider my best friend my best friend is because I can trust him. I can tell him things that I know no one else will ever find out. That's the kind of relationship we also should have with our parents. One of the greatest kinds of pain we can experience is to tell someone whom we love a deep and precious secret and then discover he told someone else. Love always trusts; and where there is no trust, there is no love.

Love Hopes

Love also comes with hope. If I love you, then I'm always hoping for the best, hoping for something better. You already know that my grandfather was an alcoholic. My cousin and I knew where he kept his bottle of gin. Because he was always drunk, he often had memory lapses. Every now and then we would take his bottle and hide it in the milk box. He'd look and look for the bottle and get angry because he couldn't find it. But soon he discovered that we were the pranksters. Then he always approached us to find out what we had done with his bottle. As I analyze what we did, we were not only playing with our grandfather but were, in fact, hoping that one day he would not find the bottle and, perhaps, spend that day without drinking. That was a weird kind of love we had for our grandfather, but we always hoped for the best.

Someone in your family may be on drugs; may be an alcoholic; or may have a disease. No matter how bad his condition is, there is an attitude of hope when love is present. Where there is love there is a desire that things will get better.

Love Perseveres

Love not only hopes, it also perseveres. Perseverance is related to faith. Think about what your mother went through the day you were born. When I went to the hospital with my wife the night before our babies were born, she was in such pain I hardly recognized her. We had gone to classes that taught us what to do when labor pains began. We knew the proper exercises. There was a role I was supposed to play when labor began. There was breathing that both of us were supposed to do. I was instructed to hold her hand. We practiced all these steps a number of times.

But her pain was so obviously excruciating that when she yelled, all of what I had learned in those classes disappeared. I called the nurse, and she gave Donna medicine. I watched the agony which she endured for almost 24 hours, attempting to have the babies. This was real perseverance. My wife persevered, and she had those children in spite of the pain.

When things get tough at home, you will attempt to persevere and survive if you love your family. The result of my wife's perseverance was to have those babies. We enjoy them tremendously, but the process was very painful. Similarly, the process of persevering through problems may be painful. But the results will be worth the suffering.

Love Never Fails

Finally, love never fails. Isn't that a summary of all these characteristics as well as the rest of this book? When all else fails, when no one else is there, the one who loves me will be around even if I'm wrong. Your family may be driving you crazy, but real love will prompt you to hang in there until the problems turn into blessings. It will help you move from survival to satisfaction at home. Are you ready to try it?

Family Focus

1. Review the following characteristics of love. Then place a check mark before the ones you are practicing at home. Place an X before the ones you need to work on.

Real love
___ is patient

___ is kind
___ does not envy
___ does not boast
___ is not proud
___ is not rude
___ is not self-seeking
___ is not easily angered
___ keeps no record of wrongs
___ does not delight in evil
___ rejoices with the truth
___ always protects
___ always trusts
___ always hopes
___ always perseveres
___ never fails

2. In what practical ways can you demonstrate love to your parents or guardians? To your brothers or sisters?

3. How has your family life improved as a result of your reading this book and practicing its teachings?